Caring Connections

PHILIP J. NOORDMANS

CRC Publications
Grand Rapids, Michigan

Acknowledgments

We are grateful to Philip J. Noordmans for writing this course. He is minister of education at the Faith Reformed Church, Traverse City, Michigan.

The Scripture quotations in his publication are from the Holy Bible, New International Version. © 1973, 1978, 1984 International Bible Society. Used by permission of Zondervan Bible Publishers.

Copyright © 1996 by CRC Publications, 2850 Kalamazoo SE, Grand Rapids, Michigan 49560.

All rights reserved. With the exception of brief excerpts for review purposes, no part of this book may be reproduced in any manner whatsoever without written permission from the publisher.

Printed in the United States of America on recycled paper. ♳

Library of Congress Cataloging-in-Publication Data

Noordmans, Philip J., 1950-

    Caring connections / Philip J. Noordmans.

      p. cm. — (Acts 2 for small groups)

    ISBN 1-56212-158-8

    1. Caring—Religious aspects—Christianity. 2. Church group work. I. Title. II. Series.

BV4647.S9N66   1996

268'.434—dc20   95-51519
                                                                                                             CIP

10 9 8 7 6 5 4 3 2 1

CONTENTS

Introduction 5

Session 1   Caring 13

Session 2   Loving and Trusting 19

Session 3   Supporting 27

Session 4   Mentoring 33

Session 5   Confronting and Correcting 39

Session 6   Reconciling .45

Session 7   Reaching Out 53

Appendix A Group Goals Planning Sheet 61

INTRODUCTION

How can I build stronger relationships with my family, friends, and coworkers? With the members of my small group? With my neighbors? In other words, how can I display a Christlike love to others?

Caring Connections, a seven-session course for small groups, explores these questions. Its goal is building relationships that embody Christian care, love, prayer support, mentoring, correction, reconciliation, and outreach. Its basis is a study of several relationships in the Bible, including those of David and Jonathan, Paul and Timothy, Dorcas and her friends, and others.

Caring Connections is part of the *Acts 2* program for small groups. That program is described in detail below.

WHAT ARE *ACTS 2* SMALL GROUPS?

Acts 2 small groups look and act much like the early church house groups portrayed in Acts 2:42-47. These groups were involved in teaching, fellowship, worship, prayer, enfolding, ministry, social time, and evangelism. All of these features are basic to the life of the church. The more these characteristics define a church's small groups, the more they will also define the larger congregation.

Acts 2 groups consist of three to fifteen people who are committed to meeting regularly together to support each other and explore some aspect of the Christian life. Six important features characterize an effective *Acts 2* small group.

MAJOR FEATURES OF *ACTS 2* SMALL GROUPS

BUILDING CHRISTIAN COMMUNITY

Acts 2 groups are more than study groups; study is only one of several important activities. The basic purpose of an *Acts 2* group is to build Christian community by developing meaningful relationships among group members. All of us long to be loved and cared for in an accepting and supportive environment. A good group fosters a level of trust and safety that makes intimacy possible. A healthy *Acts 2* group will meet relational needs by sharing realities of life, praying with and for each other, ministering side by side, and having fun together.

FORMATTED MATERIALS

Each *Acts 2* meeting includes five main segments:

- Opening share time
- Bible discovery
- Reflection
- Prayer
- Planning for ministry

Groups that follow this format are likely to succeed. If these five elements are not deliberately built into each meeting, groups may shortchange themselves by inadvertently omitting, for example, silent reflection or ministry planning. The *Acts 2* materials provide a regular format that will ensure coverage of each element in all meetings.

TRAINED LEADERS

Ineffective leadership is the primary cause of failure in small groups. Qualified *Acts 2* leaders are trained, supported, and held accountable for what happens in their group.

Training workshops are available to churches that use this strategy and materials (contact CRC Publications for details). After the training workshop and before starting their own *Acts 2* groups in their local church, leaders experience an *Acts 2* group. This training teaches them the fundamentals of small group leadership by seeing and by doing.

In addition to training leaders, each church is urged to hold regular meetings for small groups leaders. These meetings grant leaders the opportunity to enhance their leadership skills, learn from each other's insights and frustrations, report progress, and support each other. The leaders' group becomes, in essence, a support group for the leaders. Trained, supported small group leaders are much more likely to be effective.

GROWTH AND REPRODUCTION

Not many small groups have an outward focus. Small groups often become ingrown and self-serving, a holy huddle that shuts out concerns of nonmembers. To break this pattern, a small group must deliberately reach out. We suggest placing an empty chair at all your meetings to remind you of the next person God will bring to the group. Group members can pray for and seek persons to fill that chair. In addition, the group may sponsor or attend "fishing pool" events to identify and connect with potential new members. *Acts 2* groups aspire to grow and reproduce a new daughter group every two to three years.

New additions should always be a group decision. Members need the approval of the whole group before inviting someone. New persons who attend should always start on a trial basis. If they don't fit the group, they should be encouraged to look for another group where they are more comfortable.

When *Acts 2* groups form new groups, the leader selects two or three members, including an apprentice leader, to be the core of the new group. The group then commissions them to form the new group and sends them off with a blessing. If other members of the group want to join this new group, they are free to do so, if invited.

MINISTRY ORIENTATION

James advises us "do not merely listen to the word.... Do what it says" (James 1:22). A small group who studies the Bible is in a good position to begin doing what it says. *Acts 2* groups do ministry as well as talk about it.

All members should be active in one or more of the tasks needed to maintain the group:

- Leader
- Assistant or apprentice leader
- Host or hostess
- Prayer leader
- Service project coordinator
- Outreach facilitator or social activity coordinator

In addition, all are encouraged to pray for persons who might join the group or those who simply need prayers. All members are also encouraged to become involved in planned group service projects.

LEADER-RECRUITED GROUPS

Assigning people to groups may be the simplest and easiest way to start a cluster of small groups, but this method seldom works. Training several leaders and sending them to find their own group members is much more effective. When a few of the invitees have accepted, the leader seeks their input in further choices. The group grows gradually as potential members respond to specific invitations. Groups that form this way are much more likely to bond, since they have chosen each other. They will also continue inviting others.

A church using this approach is likely to have a higher percentage of people involved in small groups than those using other methods. First, people sometimes say "no" to small groups because they fear being placed with people they don't like. The personal leader-recruiting system gives them more control over those with whom they will be grouped. Second, many people who will not respond to a public solicitation will respond to a personal invitation; this is especially true if the invitation comes from someone they know.

COORDINATED BY A DIRECTOR

Every local church with a small group program should have a director or coordinator of small groups. The director should schedule and lead regular leaders' meetings. He or she will receive reports from the leaders and hold them accountable to the goals that they have set. The director should also visit each of the small groups two or three times a year and give the leader an outsider's perspective on the group.

The director, as servant-leader, should build a relationship with each small group leader or leader couple in order to extend the needed support and encouragement. He or she should be available to assist them in formulating goals and plans, identifying and recruiting apprentice leaders, and finding new members. The director should also be plugged into the church's greeting and welcoming systems and be able to channel the names of church visitors to small group leaders.

WHAT HAPPENS IN A *ACTS 2* GROUP?

One *Acts 2* small group I attended went like this.

Guests began arriving about ten minutes early for the 7:00 meeting. On their way to the family room, they helped themselves to beverages and snacks set out by the hostess. Every person who arrived was greeted cordially, and we chatted about everyday things.

At about 7:05, the leader started the meeting, although everyone had not yet arrived. He asked a group member to read the first of the opening share questions. Responses were lively and numerous.

Another couple arrived and was welcomed by the group. For their benefit, the leader explained where we were in the session. The group continued sharing, moving on to the second (and more personal) of the sharing questions.

Our leader explained that some of the things we had been talking about were also addressed in today's Bible study. Someone read the opening comments and the Scripture passage. The leader read the first question and invited responses. We spent about twenty-five minutes digging into the Bible passages, using the discovery questions provided and asking some of our own questions. Twice our leader referred us to the "Helpful Notes" provided in the lesson. The study ended with the leader's summary of the main ideas.

A brief reflection time came next. Everyone worked individually and in silence as we wrote our personal responses to the four reflection questions. We had a chance to think about our personal relationship with God and to prepare for the question that preceded the prayer time: "How do I want the group to pray for me?"

Before we prayed together, most of us shared some joys and concerns. We mentioned needs in the lives of hurting persons we knew. Though some of us were a bit nervous about the prayer time, the leader put us at ease by starting us out with one-word prayers of praise. He began with "Father God, we praise you for . . ." and we completed the sentence by naming a dozen or more qualities of God. Next came "Father, we thank you for . . ." and we finished the sentence with short expressions of gratitude. Finally we said one or two sentence prayers of intercession. Someone remembered to pray for the person who would fill our empty chair. This was a comfortable and stimulating time.

The last thing we did was plan for ministry. We started by identifying three unchurched persons who would be on our prayer list. We added two singles who were fringe members of our church and a young couple who were just beginning to attend. We agreed that each of us would pray for each listed person a couple of times each week.

We made no progress on planning a "fishing pool" event, but we did decide to ask the pastor for a list of those attending the church's new member class. We also chose to take on one service project during the year. One couple agreed to lead this.

After the formal meeting, we took more refreshments and continued to visit with each other. Some group members left almost immediately. Two couples lingered for another half hour.

FUNDAMENTALS OF SMALL GROUP LIFE

FIVE BASIC FUNCTIONS

A good group will ordinarily include

A social/recreational time. Fun time is a natural and important part of the life of the group. Activities apart from the regular meetings develop stronger group relationships and especially benefit the children of the families involved.

Life-application Bible study. The questions in the Bible study section of each lesson will help you discover what the Bible says. The application element is particularly important. People tend to lose interest in abstract discussions that do not relate to their lives.

Meaningful prayer time. Everyone should have a chance to share joys and concerns and contribute to the prayer time. Not everyone is expected to pray out loud, but everyone should be allowed to do so. Don't be afraid of periods of silence—during these times, individuals may pray silently or simply bow before God in silence. The prayer time may also be a time for worship—simply focusing on God and rejoicing in his goodness.

Regular share opportunities. The Christian life is meant to be a shared life. The New Testament emphasizes that Christians come to know each other well enough to bear each other's burdens, teach and admonish one another, and even confess faults to each other. This will happen best in a small group if members are free to share with the group what life is really like for them. Of course, what is shared *must* be kept confidential.

Ministry opportunities. Every believer has at least one spiritual gift. A small group is a wonderful place to use that gift and to find support. Don't let your small group become another sit-and-soak experience—the church already has enough of those.

GROUP PATTERNS

The best place for a group to meet is in a familiar, informal setting. Around a kitchen table or a family room is ideal. Groups that meet weekly will have the most impact, but meeting weekly may not be realistic. Most groups meet biweekly or twice a month. Groups that meet less frequently lose the continuity necessary to build relationships. Biweekly meetings can be a little longer than weekly meetings but should be kept under two hours.

Each group should set growth and ministry activity goals and keep a record of its progress in meeting the set goals. Some things simply will not happen unless plans are laid and progress is regularly reviewed. Groups should try to spin off a new small group every two to three years. (See "Group Goals Planning Sheet" on page 61.)

LEADERSHIP RESPONSIBILITY

The leader's primary responsibility is to organize and lead the regular small group meeting. This means facilitating involvement of people in sharing, prayer, and Bible study and working to keep a healthy balance between these various elements. A good balance of available time is as follows:

- About 25% on sharing. *Acts 2* material suggests sharing before the Bible study and before the prayer time.
- About 25% on prayer. Initially you will probably not spend this much time in prayer; as the group members come to know each other, however, this time will likely increase.
- About 40% on Bible study.
- About 10% on ministry planning.

Use the marginal notes addressed to the leader as helps to involve members in the various activities.

Between meetings, leaders should pray regularly for group members and continue contact with group members. The pastoral care is the responsibility of the whole group, but the leader must see that it is done.

Every leader should also identify an apprentice leader. This person can assist in leadership functions and prepare to lead a new, spin-off group.

Leaders should spend several hours preparing for each meeting. Be thoroughly familiar with the main theme, the Bible passages, and the directions in the material. Prepare for each question (for some, perhaps you'd rather substitute your own questions). Highlight key phrases or words for easy reference during the meeting. Develop extra questions that can help the group probe an area that needs attention. Prepare your heart as well as your thoughts. Above all, blanket the group and the time you will spend together with prayer, asking God to direct and protect you and to make himself known through his Word and Spirit.

COMMON PROBLEMS TO AVOID

Following are problems common to small groups. Any can severely diminish the effectiveness of a group or even kill it.

Shallow relationships. Sharing our ideas but not ourselves, praying for others while hiding our own pain, applying the Bible truths generally but avoiding specific personal application—these behaviors will yield shallow relationships. An increasing amount of honesty and openness are necessary in order to develop deep and meaningful relationships.

Overly intellectual discussions. Dealing only with the intellectual dimensions hinders spiritual growth and the development of Christian community. Try to spend at least half of your group study time relating biblical truths to our daily lives.

Unused gifts. A small group is a perfect place to identify, confirm, and use spiritual gifts. Groups in which one or two persons take charge do not promote gift development. Leaders are encouraged to share responsibility so that everyone is involved and challenged to use his or her gifts.

Problem members. Compulsive talkers, tangent-chasers, judgmental persons, pity-seekers, or domineering individuals can ruin a group. For the good of the group, leaders must deal with problem members lovingly but firmly.

Lack of confidentiality. Few things will shut down personal sharing faster than breaches of confidentiality. Be sure to regularly review the ground rules for preserving confidentiality and deal quickly with any compromise of these standards.

Little meaningful prayer. Perfunctory or impersonal prayers, quick opening and closing prayers, and prayers that do not touch our real lives will stultify a group. Prayer is one place where people can really connect with each other.

Holy huddles. Groups who focus inwardly soon become cliques or "holy huddles." An intimate, close-knit group is not a clique as long as it looks to the interests of others as well as its own. An exclusive small group that shuts out the cares and concerns of others has a problem.

GETTING STARTED

After appropriate training, leaders should make a list of whom they would like to have in their group. The list should include twice the number needed, since only half of those invited are likely to accept.

The next step is to prioritize the list and extend invitations to those on top of the list. Give invitations with full explanation; ask people simply to try the group. Their decision to join is not final until they have experienced at least two meetings. Those who accept the initial invitation may help choose additional group members.

When six to eight persons have accepted the initial invitation, set a date, time, and place for the first meeting. I suggest making the first meeting a social evening at which people get acquainted and are informed about the purpose and format of the group. They may also be asked at this time what they would like to study. Be prepared, however, to make a suggestion rather than to leave it wide open. Most new groups will welcome the leader's recommendation of material to be used. Give them plenty of time to ask questions too.

VALUE TO THE CHURCH

Small groups are of great value to the church. They provide a good place to grow. They're like greenhouses, shutting out the cold and letting in the light necessary for growth.

Small groups also decentralize caregiving. Small group members who know each other's needs and have regular contact can minister to each other in a way that diminishes the need for attention by paid staff.

Furthermore, small groups break a natural path for evangelism, assimilation, and discipleship. Relationships draw people to Christ, bring them into the church, and help them mature. Relationships are the primary strength of the small group.

Starting and maintaining a good small group program is not a quick and easy task. It requires gifted people, solid training, and constant administrative attention. Above all, it requires the grace and power of God released through prayer.

Acts 2 groups reflect the realities of the Acts 2:42-47 experience in which early Christians "devoted themselves to the apostles' teaching and to fellowship, to the breaking of bread and to prayer" and in which "believers had everything in common . . . gave to anyone as he had need . . . ate together with glad and sincere hearts . . . and added to their number daily."

Alvin J. Vander Griend
Minister of Evangelism Resources
Christian Reformed Church Home Missions

Session 1
CARING

OPENING SHARE TIME
10-15 minutes

Sharing is an important function of *Acts 2* small groups. Your relationships with others in the group will deepen as you share honestly and openly and maintain confidentiality.

1. Give an example of caring/compassion from your community or church that you've heard about recently.

2. Complete this sentence: "I feel cared for when..."

> **Leader:** Go around the circle, giving each person an opportunity to respond. If time is limited, use only the second question. Beginning with your own responses may be helpful to the group.

BIBLE DISCOVERY TIME
20-30 minutes

"Hi! How are you?"

"Fine. You?"

"Great."

Familiar greetings such as this comprise a necessary part of our social fabric, but they often indicate politeness more than authentic interaction. Most of us long for something more—for sincere, caring, compassionate relationships.

Read Acts 9:36-43. In this passage a person who cared is honored.

> *Ask one or two group members to read the introductory comments and the Bible passage. Lead the group in discussing the questions that follow the passage.*

> ³⁶*In Joppa there was a disciple named Tabitha (which, when translated, is Dorcas), who was always doing good and helping the poor.* ³⁷*About that time she became sick and died, and her body was washed and placed in an upstairs room.* ³⁸*Lydda was near Joppa; so when the disciples heard that Peter was in Lydda, they sent two men to him and urged him, "Please come at once!"*
>
> ³⁹*Peter went with them, and when he arrived he was taken upstairs to the room. All the widows stood around him, crying and showing him the robes and other clothing that Dorcas had made while she was still with them.*

13

⁴⁰*Peter sent them all out of the room; then he got down on his knees and prayed. Turning toward the dead woman, he said, "Tabitha, get up." She opened her eyes, and seeing Peter she sat up. ⁴¹He took her by the hand and helped her to her feet. Then he called the believers and the widows and presented her to them alive. ⁴²This became known all over Joppa, and many people believed in the Lord. ⁴³Peter stayed in Joppa for some time with a tanner named Simon.*

Helpful Notes
- *Joppa.* A seaport about 38 miles from Jerusalem. Today it is called Jaffa and is near Tel Aviv.
- *Come at once.* Peter was urged to hurry in order to arrive before Dorcas was buried.

> Leader: Refer to "Helpful Notes" when they pertain to your discussion. You may want to ask a group member to read these notes aloud.

1. If Dorcas were a member of your congregation, what kinds of things would she be doing? For whom?
2. What words and actions show how deeply Peter and the others loved Dorcas?
3. What can we learn from this passage about our relationships with others?

Read Luke 10:25-37. In this powerful story Jesus teaches us how we are to love our neighbors as ourselves.

> Consider presenting this passage as reader's theater. Ask someone to read the lines spoken by the expert in the law. A second person can read Jesus' lines, and a third person can be the narrator, reading the lines that are not in quotation marks.

²⁵On one occasion an expert in the law stood up to test Jesus. "Teacher," he asked, "what must I do to inherit eternal life?"

²⁶"What is written in the Law?" he replied. "How do you read it?"

²⁷He answered, " 'Love the Lord your God with all your heart and with all your soul and with all your strength and with all your mind'; and 'Love your neighbor as yourself.' "

²⁸"You have answered correctly," Jesus replied. "Do this and you will live."

²⁹But he wanted to justify himself, so he asked Jesus, "And who is my neighbor?"

³⁰In reply Jesus said, "A man was going down from Jerusalem to Jericho, when he fell into the hands of robbers. They stripped him of his clothes, beat him and went away, leaving him half dead. ³¹A priest happened to be going down the same road, and when he saw the man, he passed by on the other side. ³²So, too, a Levite, when he came to the place and saw him, passed by on the other side. ³³But a Samaritan, as he traveled, came where the man was; and when he saw him, he took pity on him. ³⁴He went to him and bandaged his wounds, pouring on oil and wine. Then he put the man on his own donkey, took him to an inn and took care of him. ³⁵The next day he took out two silver coins and gave them to the innkeeper. 'Look after him,' he said, 'and when I return, I will reimburse you for any extra expense you may have.'

³⁶"Which of these three do you think was a neighbor to the man who fell into the hands of robbers?"

³⁷The expert in the law replied, "The one who had mercy on him."

Jesus said to him, "Go and do likewise."

Helpful Notes
- *Love the Lord . . . Love your neighbor.* Jesus uses these words to reply to a question put to him by another "expert on the law." His question was, "Which is the greatest commandment?" See Matthew 22:34-40.
- *To justify himself.* Perhaps the expert on the law wanted to justify his lack of love for some kinds of people, so he asks Jesus which neighbors he should love.
- *Priest . . . Levite.* The two travelers represent the religious professionals (priests) and their lay associates (Levites).
- *Samaritan.* The Jews to whom Jesus was speaking hated Samaritans, regarding them as inferior "half-breeds." No Jew would talk to or associate with a Samaritan. The Samaritans usually returned the ill will.

1. Why do you suppose the priest and the Levite passed by the wounded man?
2. What motivated the Samaritan to help him?
3. Who, according to this parable, are our neighbors? How are we to love them as ourselves?

Leader: Ask someone to read the main ideas slowly and thoughtfully. Do the same with the "Good News" section.

MAIN IDEAS

- People who serve others develop rich, meaningful relationships with them.
- God calls us to love our neighbors as ourselves.
- Our neighbors are persons near us who are in need.
- Compassion crosses ethnic, social, and economic barriers to genuinely care for those in need.

GOOD NEWS

As believers, we are "cared for" people. And we, in turn, lovingly care for those in need.

REFLECTION TIME

7-10 minutes

Group members work individually during the reflection time. Jot down your own personal responses to reflection questions. You may want to point out that our reflection time and prayer time usually include praise or thanksgiving, confession, requests or petitions for ourselves, and intercession for others.

Jot down your personal reflections, using the questions below.

1. Praise God for people like Dorcas who have served you.

2. Whom can I serve in some way this week? What should I ask God for concerning this person?

3. Do I need to ask God to forgive anything concerning my relationship with others?

4. How do I want the group to pray for me?

PRAYER TIME

PREPARATION
5-10 minutes

You are invited to share any answers or parts of answers from questions 1-4. Share especially those insights that will help the group pray meaningfully with you and for you.

PRAYER
10-15 minutes

Begin with prayers of thanks/praise for ways that fellow believers have served you in the past.

Continue by praying for any needs mentioned during the preparation time.

Feel free to contribute more than once.

Expect some times of silence. Use them to listen to the Spirit or to offer a silent prayer.

After several minutes, the leader will close the prayer time.

Leader: Go around the circle, giving each person an opportunity to share his or her response to one or two of the reflection questions. Encourage members to mention ways that you as a group can pray for them.

Ask a group member to read these guidelines before the prayer time begins. Initially you may spend considerably less than the allotted time in prayer, but as the group grows closer, the prayer time should expand.

PLANNING FOR MINISTRY

Service or ministry is an important function of *Acts 2* small groups. This section will suggest some ways that your group can plan for ministry.

Begin by establishing some goals for the group. Discuss each goal and consider its value to your group and to your church before you set the goal. Be sure the goals are something you can accomplish.

If your group has been meeting for some time, review the group's goals and make any necessary revisions or additions.

Refer the group to Appendix A—Group Goals Planning Sheet.

Session 2
LOVING AND TRUSTING

OPENING SHARE TIME
10-15 minutes

Sharing is an important function of *Acts 2* small groups. Notice that the first share time question is general and the second is more specific and personal.

1. What qualities do you value in a friend?
2. Think of one of your best friends. How did you become friends? Why do you remain friends?

> Leader: As you go around the circle sharing responses, persons who choose not to share may simply say "pass." Tell the group members that this is always an acceptable response.

BIBLE DISCOVERY TIME
20-30 minutes

In a world filled with distorted relationships and dysfunctional families, we need models of deeper, healthier friendships. David's friendship with Jonathan provides such a model.

Read 1 Samuel 18:1-5. Having just killed Goliath, young David is brought to King Saul.

> Ask someone to read the introductory comments. Have someone else read the Bible passage. Lead the group in discussing the questions that follow the passage.

> After David had finished talking with Saul, Jonathan became one in spirit with David, and he loved him as himself. ²From that day Saul kept David with him and did not let him return to his father's house. ³And Jonathan made a covenant with David because he loved him as himself. ⁴Jonathan took off the robe he was wearing and gave it to David, along with his tunic, and even his sword, his bow and his belt.
>
> ⁵Whatever Saul sent him to do, David did it so successfully that Saul gave him a high rank in the army. This pleased all the people, and Saul's officers as well.

Helpful Notes
- *Gave it [the robe] to David.* According to the *NIV Study Bible*, the giving of the robe and the other items (tunic, sword, bow, belt) may indicate that Jonathan realized David would take his place as Saul's successor.

> Refer to "Helpful Notes" when they pertain to your discussion. You may want to ask a group member to read these notes aloud.

1. The New American Standard version of the Bible translates 18:1 this way: "the soul of Jonathan was knit to the soul of David." Compare this phrase to what African Americans mean by the term *soul brother*.

2. Note that Jonathan's love for David is not one-sided; David likewise loves Jonathan (see 2 Samuel 1:26). How do you react to the use of the word *love* to describe the relationship between two men?

3. Covenants (vs. 3) usually involved mutual promises of loyalty and friendship. Jonathan accepts David as his equal. In view of who Jonathan is and who David is rapidly becoming, what risks would such a friendship carry? What qualities would it need to survive?

Leader: This passage lends itself to reading in parts (reader's theater). You'll need a narrator to read the lines not in quotation marks and readers for David's lines and Jonathan's lines. Present the reading as an intense dialogue between good friends.

Read 1 Samuel 20:1-17, 41-42. David is growing immensely popular in Israel, and King Saul is becoming increasingly insecure and jealous. Saul determines that David must die. Because of his fondness for David, Jonathan negotiates a truce between his father, Saul, and his friend David. But the truce does not last long; Saul again sets out to kill David.

Then David fled from Naioth at Ramah and went to Jonathan and asked, "What have I done? What is my crime? How have I wronged your father, now that he is trying to take my life?"

²"Never!" Jonathan replied. "You are not going to die! Look, my father doesn't do anything, great or small, without confiding in me. Why would he hide this from me? It's not so!"

³But David took an oath and said, "Your father knows very well that I have found favor in your eyes, and he has said to himself, 'Jonathan must not know this or he will be grieved.' Yet as surely as the LORD lives and as you live, there is only a step between me and death."

⁴Jonathan said to David, "Whatever you want me to do, I'll do it for you."

⁵So David said, "Look, tomorrow is the New Moon festival, and I am supposed to dine with the king; but let me go and hide in the field until the evening of the day after tomorrow. ⁶If your father misses me at all, tell him, 'David earnestly asked my permission to hurry to Bethlehem, his hometown, because an annu-

al sacrifice is being made there for his whole clan.' ⁷If he says, 'Very well,' then your servant is safe. But if he loses his temper, you can be sure that he is determined to harm me. ⁸As for you, show kindness to your servant, for you have brought him into a covenant with you before the Lord. If I am guilty, then kill me yourself. Why hand me over to your father?"

⁹"Never," Jonathan said. "If I had the least inkling that my father was determined to harm you, wouldn't I tell you?"

¹⁰David asked, "Who will tell me if your father answers you harshly?"

¹¹"Come," Jonathan said, "let's go out into the field." So they went there together.

¹²Then Jonathan said to David: "By the Lord, the God of Israel, I will surely sound out my father by this time the day after tomorrow! If he is favorably disposed toward you, will I not send you word and let you know? ¹³But if my father is inclined to harm you, may the Lord deal with me, be it ever so severely, if I do not let you know and send you away safely. May the Lord be with you as he has been with my father. ¹⁴But show me unfailing kindness like that of the Lord as long as I live, so that I may not be killed, ¹⁵and do not ever cut off your kindness from my family—not even when the Lord has cut off every one of David's enemies from the face of the earth."

¹⁶So Jonathan made a covenant with the house of David, saying, "May the Lord call David's enemies to account." ¹⁷And Jonathan had David reaffirm his oath out of love for him, because he loved him as he loved himself.

[Note: Verses 18-40 tell how Saul's anger flared at David and at Jonathan. Jonathan gives David a pre-arranged signal informing him of his father's anger, and the two say goodbye.]

⁴¹David . . . bowed down before Jonathan three times, with his face to the ground. Then they kissed each other and wept together—but David wept the most.

⁴²Jonathan said to David, "Go in peace, for we have sworn friendship with each other in the name of the Lord, saying, 'The Lord is witness between you and me, and between your descendants and my descen-

dants forever.' " Then David left and Jonathan went back to the town.

Helpful Notes
- *That I may not be killed.* Jonathan is asking David to spare his life when David comes into power. It was common practice for new rulers to kill all potential rivals for the throne.
- *Call David's enemies to account.* Jonathan undoubtedly realizes that his father may well be among those "called to account." Jonathan's loyalties lie with his friend.

1. How do the first three verses show that David trusts Jonathan?

2. Besides *trust,* what other words would you use to characterize their relationship? Explain your choices.

Leader: Continue the reader's theater format for this final passage. No new readers are needed.

Read 1 Samuel 23:14-18. Saul has continued to hound David. In this passage, David and Jonathan meet for a final time.

> ¹⁴*David stayed in the desert strongholds and in the hills of the Desert of Ziph. Day after day Saul searched for him, but God did not give David into his hands.*
>
> ¹⁵*While David was at Horesh in the Desert of Ziph, he learned that Saul had come out to take his life.* ¹⁶*And Saul's son Jonathan went to David at Horesh and helped him find strength in God.* ¹⁷*"Don't be afraid,"* he said. *"My father Saul will not lay a hand on you. You will be king over Israel, and I will be second to you. Even my father Saul knows this."* ¹⁸*The two of them made a covenant before the* LORD. *Then Jonathan went home, but David remained at Horesh.*

1. What qualities of friendship do you find in this scene?

2. Compare what Jonathan was willing to do for David with what many contemporary motivational speakers exhort us to do for ourselves.

MAIN IDEAS

Ask someone to read the main ideas slowly and thoughtfully. Do the same with the "Good News" section.

Deep, healthy, David-Jonathan friendships are a gift from God and are characterized by:

- Affirmation (1 Sam. 18:1-5; 23:17). True friends recognize your potential; they affirm what you are becoming.

- Love (1 Sam. 18:1, 3; 20:17; 2 Sam. 1:26). Friends love one another. To love others is to contemplate what is truly best for them and to offer that "best" to them. Friends seek one another's highest good.
- Loyalty (1 Sam. 20:16-17; 42; 23:18). Friends remain loyal to one another in spite of geographic separation and danger.
- Trust (1 Sam. 20:1-3). Friends trust one another and fear no betrayal.
- Encouragement (1 Sam. 23:16). Friends help friends find strength in God.

GOOD NEWS

With God's help, we can develop loving, David-Jonathan relationships in our own lives. The Christian community is a rich source of such relationships.

REFLECTION TIME

5-7 minutes

Jot down your personal reflections, using the following questions:

1. For what David-Jonathan relationships in my life can I thank and praise God?

2. Do I long for an improved relationship with anybody? What should I ask for that person and for myself?

Leader: Group members work individually during the reflection time. Point out that these personal, written reflections can guide our prayers during the week as well as during this meeting.

3. In light of our study of David and Jonathan's friendship, how can we as a group pray for you? For what do you long?

PRAYER TIME

PREPARATION

5-10 minutes

Leader: Go around the circle, giving each person an opportunity to share his or her response to one or two of the reflection questions.

You are invited to share any answers or parts of answers from questions 1-3, above. Share especially those insights that will help the group pray meaningfully with you and for you.

PRAYER

10-15 minutes

Ask a group member to read these guidelines before the prayer time begins. Appoint someone to close the prayer time.

Consider beginning with a song of praise such as "What a Friend We Have in Jesus."

Stand in a circle, join hands, and encourage one another in the Lord by praying for one another. Give thanks for each other and for the bonds the group is developing.

Pray for any needs that group members mention.

Pray for openness to new persons God may lead to your group.

Contribute more than once, if you wish. Don't be afraid to repeat what someone else has said. Use silence to listen to the Spirit or to offer a silent prayer.

PLANNING FOR MINISTRY

Discuss the "empty chair" strategy with your group. This implies a deliberate outward focus and a desire to grow. Is the group willing to commit to this?

Service or ministry is an important function of *Acts 2* small groups. This section will suggest some ways that your group can plan for ministry.

If you haven't already done so, set an empty chair in your circle at your next meeting. The chair can serve as a constant reminder of the next person God will bring into the group. Group members can pray for and actively seek persons to occupy that chair.

Compile (or renew) a list of potential new group members. Include persons who are unchurched, undiscipled, or inactive members of your own congregation. Decide who will keep the list, add available information, and distribute the list to the group for prayer. Begin intercession.

Session 3
SUPPORTING

OPENING SHARE TIME
10-15 minutes

Sharing is an important function of *Acts 2* small groups. Notice that the first share time question is general and the second is more specific and personal.

1. Mention some words or phrases people typically use to communicate that they are "standing with you" or supporting you.

2. Tell the group about a time when you needed people to pray for you.

Leader: It's easy to allow the personal sharing time to go too long, so that you have to cut back on other parts. Stay within your time limits.

BIBLE DISCOVERY TIME
20-30 minutes

Life is lonely for the unconnected. God designed us to be linked to him and to one another and to draw strength from our bonds of love. Prayer is one way we can support one another.

Read Acts 12:1-19. In this passage the newly-formed church prays for one of its leaders who is in prison.

Ask someone to read the introductory comments. Then take turns reading the Bible passage. Anyone who is uncomfortable reading aloud may say "pass." Lead the group in discussing the questions that follow the passage.

> *It was about this time that King Herod arrested some who belonged to the church, intending to persecute them. ²He had James, the brother of John, put to death with the sword. ³When he saw that this pleased the Jews, he proceeded to seize Peter also. This happened during the Feast of Unleavened Bread. ⁴After arresting him, he put him in prison, handing him over to be guarded by four squads of four soldiers each. Herod intended to bring him out for public trial after the Passover.*
>
> *⁵So Peter was kept in prison, but the church was earnestly praying to God for him.*
>
> *⁶The night before Herod was to bring him to trial, Peter was sleeping between two soldiers, bound with two chains, and sentries stood guard at the entrance. ⁷Suddenly an angel of the Lord appeared and a light shone in the cell. He struck Peter on the side and woke*

him up. "Quick, get up!" he said, and the chains fell off Peter's wrists.

⁸Then the angels said to him, "Put on your clothes and sandals." And Peter did so. "Wrap your cloak around you and follow me," the angel told him.

⁹Peter followed him out of the prison, but he had no idea that what the angel was doing was really happening; he thought he was seeing a vision. ¹⁰They passed the first and second guards and came to the iron gate leading to the city. It opened for them by itself, and they went through it. When they had walked the length of one street, suddenly the angel left him.

¹¹Then Peter came to himself and said, "Now I know without a doubt that the Lord sent his angel and rescued me from Herod's clutches and from everything the Jewish people were anticipating."

¹²When this had dawned on him, he went to the house of Mary the mother of John, also called Mark, where many people had gathered and were praying. ¹³Peter knocked at the outer entrance, and a servant girl named Rhoda came to answer the door. ¹⁴When she recognized Peter's voice, she was so overjoyed she ran back without opening it and exclaimed, "Peter is at the door!"

¹⁵"You're out of your mind," they told her. When she kept insisting that it was so, they said, "It must be his angel."

¹⁶But Peter kept on knocking, and when they opened the door and saw him, they were astonished. ¹⁷Peter motioned with his hand for them to be quiet and described how the Lord had brought him out of prison. "Tell James and the brothers about this," he said, and then he left for another place.

¹⁸In the morning, there was no small commotion among the soldiers as to what had become of Peter. ¹⁹After Herod had a thorough search made for him and did not find him, he cross-examined the guards and ordered that they be executed.

1. Underline words and phrases that communicate Herod's intent.

2. What miracles occurred in this story?

3. What does this passage teach about angels? (See also Acts 12:23.)

4. Who organized the prayer meeting? How long did it last? Who attended it? What would it have been like to be present?

5. What can we learn about prayer from this passage?

   Helpful Notes
   - *James, the brother of John.* Not the James who was the Lord's brother and a leader in the Jerusalem church (Acts 12:17), but James the brother of John (Matthew 4:21).
   - *Four squads of four soldiers each.* Peter was not guarded by sixteen soldiers at once, but by groups of four soldiers, one for each watch of the night.
   - *They were astonished.* Confronted with a direct answer to their prayers, the believers at first reject the evidence as the figment of a disturbed mind, then attribute it to an angel who resembled Peter, and, finally, are astonished by it! The writer of Acts wants us to catch the irony and humor in this situation.

Leader: Refer to "Helpful Notes" when they pertain to your discussion. You may want to ask a group member to read these notes aloud.

MAIN IDEAS

- We all, at times, "stand in the need of prayer."
- We need to support one another in prayer.
- We should pray in faith, believing that God is able to answer our prayer (sometimes in surprising ways).
- Faithful, earnest prayers make a difference in our lives. The ministry of prayer is vital.
- Gathering to pray with other Christians should be an important part of our prayer lives.

Ask someone to read the main ideas slowly and thoughtfully. Be open to additional ideas group members offer.

GOOD NEWS

The prayers of God's people support us in our times of need.

REFLECTION TIME

5-7 minutes

Leader: Group members work individually during the reflection time. Given today's topic of praying for one another, encourage group members to focus especially on question 4.

Jot down your personal reflections, using the questions below.

1. What did I learn about prayer that prompts me to praise and thank God?

2. Should I be praying for someone inside or outside of our group? If so, for what should I ask God?

3. Is my own prayer life what it should be?

4. How do I want this group to pray for me?

PRAYER TIME

PREPARATION

5-10 minutes

You may want to jot down (on a sheet of newsprint) the personal needs the group members mention. Consult the sheet during the prayer time.

You are invited to share any answers or parts of answers from questions 1-4, above. Especially share any ways the group can pray for you today and during the week.

PRAYER

10-15 minutes

Ask a group member to read through these guidelines before the prayer time begins. To set up for the prayer time, place an empty chair in the middle of the room. Ask the group to stand in a circle around the chair.

You may want to begin your prayer time by singing a song that asks God to hear our prayer; for example, "Hear Our Prayer, O Lord," or "Lord, Listen to Your Children Praying."

Each person is invited to sit in the center of the circle, one at a time. The others stand, place their hands on that person, and pray for him or her. The prayers may include and go beyond needs the person has requested. Thanks for the person and his or her presence in the group is also appropriate.

Close with a favorite song of praise or by reading a praise psalm (such as Psalm 103) responsively.

PLANNING FOR MINISTRY

Especially appropriate this week are prayers for specific needy people in the community who might be interested in joining the group.

Distribute and review your intercession list and add new names. Decide who will pray for whom.

> Leader: The ministry of prayer is vital. As a group you could plan a special time to meet to intercede for needs in your church, community, nation, and world.

Session 4
MENTORING

OPENING SHARE TIME
10-15 minutes

Are these opening share times helpful in getting to know each other? We hope so! Here are today's openers:

1. When do we serve as mentors or role models to others?

2. Think of someone who has acted as a role model or mentor for you, someone who positively affected your life. How did this person help you? In what ways did you change because of your relationship with him or her?

Leader: Occasionally you may want to substitute your own opening share questions (or questions from your group) for ours.

BIBLE DISCOVERY TIME
20-30 minutes

Each of us need role models, not only to hold us accountable but also to exemplify Christian virtues, spiritual maturity, and effective ministry. And we, in turn, are called to mentor the faith of fellow family members, of children and young people from the church, of a friend or group member.

Our Bible study today focuses on the apostle Paul's mentoring relationship to Timothy.

Read Acts 16:1-5. In this passage Paul invites young Timothy to join him on his second missionary journey.

> *He came to Derbe and then to Lystra, where a disciple named Timothy lived, whose mother was a Jewess and a believer, but whose father was a Greek. ²The brothers at Lystra and Iconium spoke well of him. ³Paul wanted to take him along on the journey, so he circumcised him because of the Jews who lived in that area, for they all knew that his father was a Greek. ⁴As they traveled from town to town, they delivered the decisions reached by the apostles and elders in Jerusalem for the people to obey. ⁵So the churches were strengthened in the faith and grew daily in numbers.*

Ask someone to read the introductory comments. Then take turns reading the Bible passage. Lead the group in discussing the questions that follow the passage.

Leader: Refer to "Helpful Notes" when they pertain to your discussion. You may want to ask a group member to read these notes aloud.

Helpful Notes

- *Whose mother was . . . a believer.* Though Timothy's father was not a Christian, his mother (Eunice) and his grandmother (Lois) taught him the Old Testament "from infancy" (see 2 Tim. 1:5; 3:15). Timothy may have converted to Christianity during Paul's first trip to Lystra.
- *Circumcised him.* Timothy submits to Paul's action as a means of making their ministry to the Jews more effective. His Greek ancestry might have been a liability, had he not been circumcised.

You may want to use a large map to locate the three cities cited in this passage.

1. Why do you think Paul invited young Timothy to accompany him on a missionary journey?

2. What was Timothy's role on the journey? What impact do you think this experience had on Timothy?

Read 1 Timothy 1:18-19; 4:12-16. Timothy, now in his mid-thirties or younger, has matured into a leader in the early church.

> *[18]Timothy, my son, I give you this instruction in keeping with the prophecies once made about you, so that by following them you may fight the good fight, [19]holding on to faith and a good conscience. Some have rejected these and so have shipwrecked their faith (1 Tim. 1:18-19).*
>
> *[12]Don't let anyone look down on you because you are young, but set an example for the believers in speech, in life, in love, in faith and in purity. [13]Until I come, devote yourself to the public reading of Scripture, to reaching and to teaching. [14]Do not neglect your gift, which was given you through a prophetic message, when the body of elders laid their hands on you.*
>
> *[15]Be diligent in these matters; give yourself wholly to them, so that everyone may see your progress. [16]Watch your life and doctrine closely. Persevere in them, because if you do, you will save both yourself and your hearers (1 Tim. 4:12-16).*

Helpful Notes

- *Prophecies once made about you.* Apparently, God had revealed to certain believers (prophets) that Timothy would be a leader in the church.

1. What role of a mentor do these verses illustrate?
2. What advice does Paul give that we should pass to those we mentor?
3. Has another believer ever held you accountable? If so, did you benefit from the experience? Explain.

Read Philippians 2:19-24. Paul writes this letter while a prisoner in Rome. He wants to send Timothy to visit the Philippian church.

> *¹⁹I hope in the Lord Jesus to send Timothy to you soon, that I also may be cheered when I receive news about you. ²⁰I have no one else like him, who takes a genuine interest in your welfare. ²¹For everyone looks out for his own interests, not those of Jesus Christ. ²²But you know that Timothy has proved himself, because as a son with his father he has served with me in the work of the gospel. ²³I hope, therefore, to send him as soon as I see how things go with me. ²⁴And I am confident in the Lord that I myself will come soon.*

Leader: Encourage interested group members to read Paul's two letters to Timothy for their devotions this week.

1. Describe the relationship between Paul and Timothy.
2. One way mentors teach is by direct instruction. What other method does verse 22 suggest?
3. What impact did Paul's mentoring have on Timothy?
4. How do you think Paul benefited from mentoring Timothy?
5. Who views you as their "Paul"? How do you feel about that? What are you doing to develop your "Timothy"?

MAIN IDEAS

- In some relationships we are "Paul"; in others, we are "Timothy." We both mentor and are mentored.
- Mentors hold persons accountable; they instruct others by words and by their Christian example.
- Those who are mentored learn not only by listening to their mentor's teachings, but especially by observing the mentor's life and example.
- Mentoring usually cannot be forced; both "Paul" and "Timothy" must want it.
- Good mentoring relationships result in spiritual growth.

For a change of pace, ask group members to sum up the main ideas they've received from the session so far, or have the entire group read this section and the "Good News" section in unison.

GOOD NEWS

God provides mature fellow Christians to encourage us in our faith; he also gives us opportunities to help shape the spiritual lives of others.

REFLECTION TIME

5-7 minutes

Leader: Group members work individually during the reflection time. Jot down your own personal responses to reflection questions. You may want to remind the group that our reflection time and prayer time usually include praise or thanksgiving, confession, requests for ourselves, and intercession for others.

Jot down your personal reflections, using the questions below.

1. Who are the people who have guided your spiritual life for whom you can thank and praise God?

2. Have I been a good spiritual example to those who look up to me? Do I need to ask God's forgiveness for anything?

3. Do I long for a Paul-Timothy relationship? If so, for what can I ask God?

4. Am I attempting to help anyone spiritually? How can the group pray for that person?

PRAYER TIME

PREPARATION
5-10 minutes

You are invited to share any answers or parts of answers from questions 1-4.

Leader: Go around the circle, giving each person an opportunity to share his or her response to one or two of the reflection questions.

PRAYER
10-15 minutes

Stand in a circle, join hands, and pray for one another.

Begin with one-word prayers of praise.

"Lord, I praise you for . . ."

Continue with one-phrase prayers of thanksgiving.

"Lord, I thank you for . . ."

As the Spirit leads, move into a time of confession and petition.

Contribute more than once, if you wish. Don't be afraid to repeat what someone else has said.

Use silent time to listen to the Spirit or to offer a silent prayer.

You may want to close by singing (or saying in unison) "Lord, Speak to Me That I May Speak."

Ask a group member to read these guidelines before the prayer time.

Lord, speak to me that I may speak
in living echoes of your tone.
As you have sought, so let me seek
your erring children lost and lone.

O lead me, Lord, that I may lead
the wandering and the wavering feet.
O feed me, Lord, that I may feed
your hungry ones with manna sweet.

O teach me, Lord, that I may teach
the precious truths which you impart.
And win my words that they may reach
the hidden depths of many a heart.

O use me, Lord, use even me,
just as you will, and when, and where.
Until your blessed face I see,
your rest, your joy, your glory share.

PLANNING FOR MINISTRY

Leader: In your discussion, remember that mentoring can't be forced. "Paul" and "Timothy" must both want mentoring.

You may want to discuss the following:

- To mentor or to be mentored is to be involved in ministry. Can your group members fill any mentoring needs in your congregation? For example, some congregations provide a mature adult mentor for each young teen. Others assign sponsors to individuals or families who have just joined the church.

- If new members join your group, they might appreciate a mentor or sponsor within the group.

- If existing group members feel the need to be mentored, perhaps the group could meet that need, drawing on either the group itself or contacts within the congregation.

Session 5
CONFRONTING AND CORRECTING

OPENING SHARE TIME
10-15 minutes

1. What are some ways we use the word *face* in our society?
2. Discuss a time when someone got "in your face" and challenged something you said, thought, or did.

> Leader: As an alternative to the first question below, you could discuss this statement: "Our society seems to encourage confrontation." Do you agree or disagree?

BIBLE DISCOVERY TIME
20-30 minutes

With the possible exception of Marine drill sergeants, most people don't enjoy confrontation and correction. In the Christian community, however, caring about someone means lovingly confronting and correcting him or her when necessary.

> Ask someone to read the introductory comments. Take turns reading the Bible passages. Lead the group in discussing the questions that follow the passage.

Read Galatians 2:11-16. In this passage, Paul, an apostle to the Gentiles, publicly confronts his peer, Peter, an apostle to the Jews.

> [11] When Peter came to Antioch, I [Paul] opposed him to his face, because he was clearly in the wrong. [12] Before certain men came from James, he used to eat with the Gentiles. But when they arrived, he began to draw back and separate himself from the Gentiles because he was afraid of those who belonged to the circumcision group. [13] The other Jews joined him in his hypocrisy, so that by their hypocrisy even Barnabas was led astray.
>
> [14] When I saw that they were not acting in line with the truth of the gospel, I said to Peter in front of them all, "You are a Jew, yet you live like a Gentile and not like a Jew. How is it, then, that you force Gentiles to follow Jewish customs?
>
> [15] "We who are Jews by birth and not 'Gentile sinners' [16] know that a man is not justified by observing the law, but by faith in Jesus Christ. So we, too, have put our faith in Christ Jesus that we may be justified by

faith in Christ and not by observing the law, because by observing the law no one will be justified."

Helpful Notes

Leader: Refer to "Helpful Notes" when they pertain to your discussion. You may want to refer the group to Acts 15:1-5 for additional background information.

- *Antioch.* Antioch, the chief city of Syria, was where the first Gentile church began and where the disciples were first called "Christians."
- *Came from James.* James, the brother of Jesus, was the leader of the Jerusalem church.
- *Used to eat with the Gentiles.* While living among the Gentiles, Peter apparently set aside the Jewish dietary restrictions and other customs; after the men from James came, he began practicing Jewish-style social separation. Paul rightly calls this "hypocrisy." It forced Gentile Christians to follow Jewish customs.
- *Circumcision group.* Jews who continued to follow Jewish customs even after they became Christians. They insisted that the Jewish rite of circumcision was necessary for salvation. They also taught that circumcised Jewish believers should not eat with Gentile Christians.

1. Why did Peter do what he did? What was wrong with his action?

2. Why did Paul confront Peter publicly? Couldn't he have talked to Peter in private?

3. In what settings today does public confrontation occur? In what kind of situations might this be necessary?

Read Matthew 18:15-17. In contrast to the episode we just read above, these words from Jesus are about private confrontation.

> ¹⁵"If your brother sins against you, go and show him his fault, just between the two of you. If he listens to you, you have won your brother over. ¹⁶But if he will not listen, take one or two others along, so that 'every matter may be established by the testimony of two or three witnesses.' ¹⁷If he refuses to listen to them, tell it to the church; and if he refuses to listen even to the church, treat him as you would a pagan or tax collector."

1. According to this passage, when should you privately confront your brother or sister?

2. Who or what is the implied standard against which behavior and attitudes are measured?

3. Look closely at the process outlined in these verses. What is its main intent? Do you think this is a valid process for Christians to follow today?

4. If someone sins against you and you do nothing or only talk about the problem with others, what can happen to you inwardly? In what ways might your relationship to the offending person change?

> Leader: Additional passages the group may want to check include Leviticus 19:17; Proverbs 15:31; 27:5; and Luke 17:3.

MAIN IDEAS

- Our standard for right and wrong is the Word of God.
- We should always confront or correct lovingly and tactfully, for the purpose of healing and helping the offender.
- Public sins need to be dealt with publicly; private sins, privately.
- Confrontation will not necessarily generate positive results. Yet loving, tactful confrontation can strengthen relationships.

> Have group members sum up the main ideas they've received from the session so far, or ask someone to read the summary below. Do the same for the "Good News" section.

GOOD NEWS

In Christ, God has forgiven all our offenses. We also need to forgive those who offend us and be receptive to those who lovingly correct us.

Leader: Group members work individually during the reflection time. Be sure to jot down your own personal responses to the reflection questions.

You may want to remind group members to continue using their personal reflections from this course as a prayer guide at home.

REFLECTION TIME

7-10 minutes

Jot down your personal reflections, using the questions below.

1. As you reflect on today's Scripture and its application to your life, for what can you praise and thank God?

2. Do you need to be confronted or corrected in any area of your life? Do you need to privately confess anything to God about this?

3. Do you need to lovingly confront anybody? Why? How and when will you do it? What may be the outcome for you and for him or her? How will you pray for this person this week?

4. How do you want the group to pray for you this week?

PRAYER TIME

PREPARATION

5-10 minutes

Go around the circle, giving each group member an opportunity to share his or her response to one or two of the reflection questions.

You are invited to share any answers or parts of answers from questions 1-4, above.

PRAYER

10-15 minutes

Begin with two or three minutes of silence, during which you reflect on your own need for correction and ask God for forgiveness and grace.

After the time of silence, offer short prayers of thanks and praise to God for his love, mercy, and grace. If you wish, express your praise in song. (Start singing; group members who know the song will join you.)

Move into a time of petition and intercession. Perhaps group members have requested prayers for specific persons who need correction and confrontation.

You may want to conclude by reading Psalm 51 responsively.

Leader: Ask a group member to read through these guidelines before the prayer time. Be ready to make the transitions into the various parts of the prayer time, as needed.

PLANNING FOR MINISTRY

Service or ministry is an important function of *Acts 2* small groups. Perhaps the group is already involved in some aspect of serving your community or congregation. If not, you may want to discuss taking on a service project. What could your group do that would fit the interests, gifts, schedules, and resources of group members? When could you do this? Who will take the lead?

Discuss inviting new people to the group. Do you have someone in mind? Is this the right time? Who will extend the invitation? Get group consensus before you go ahead.

You may want to suggest a few possible service projects for your group's consideration. Welcome ideas from group members as well.

Encourage group members to continue praying for persons on the intercession list, persons who might fill the empty chair.

Session 6
RECONCILING

OPENING SHARE TIME
10-15 minutes

1. Mention several areas of our society that need reconciliation.
2. To reconcile is to restore harmony to a relationship once characterized by hatred, hostility, enmity, coldness. Where do you sometimes see the need for reconciliation in your life?

Leader: As an alternative to the second question, ask group members to describe a reconciliation that they've experienced, read about, or seen on TV or film.

BIBLE DISCOVERY TIME
20-30 minutes

Creating problems—between husbands and wives, parents and children, neighbors and friends—is easy. Resolving them is much harder. The good news is that God's help and the willingness of both parties make reconciliation possible.

Today we study the lives of Jacob and Esau. The rift between them was deep and ugly, but by the end of the story, they reconcile.

Read Genesis 27:41-45. The problem begins when Jacob—the younger—tricks his father Isaac into giving him the blessing which rightly belonged to his older brother, Esau.

Ask someone to read the introductory comments. You may want to read the Bible passages in reader's theater format. The first section requires a narrator to read the lines not in quotation marks and readers for Esau's lines and Rebekah's lines.

> *⁴¹Esau held a grudge against Jacob because of the blessing his father had given him. He said to himself, "The days of mourning for my father are near; then I will kill my brother Jacob."*
>
> *⁴²When Rebekah was told what her oldest son Esau had said, she sent for her younger son Jacob and said to him, "Your brother Esau is consoling himself with the thought of killing you. ⁴³Now then, my son, do what I say: Flee at once to my brother Laban in Haran. ⁴⁴Stay with him for a while until your brother's fury subsides. ⁴⁵When your brother is no longer angry with you and forgets what you did to him, I'll send word for you to come back from there. Why should I lose both of you in one day?"*

> Leader: Refer to "Helpful Notes" when they pertain to your discussion. You may want to ask a group member to read these notes aloud.

Helpful Notes
- *Days of mourning.* Esau says that he will wait until his father Isaac dies before killing his brother Jacob.
- *Lose both of you.* If Esau killed Jacob, others in the clan would probably hunt him down. Thus Rebekah would lose both of her sons.

1. Put yourself in Esau's sandals. How would you feel toward Jacob after he cheated you out of your birthright? Note the words and phrases that describe Esau's feelings.

2. According to Rebekah, what needs to happen before Jacob and Esau can reconcile? With what aspects of her philosophy do you agree?

> Continue the reader's theater format by asking for additional volunteers to read the lines of Jacob and the messengers.

Read Genesis 32:3-21. After fleeing to his uncle Laban, Jacob works fourteen years for the right to marry Laban's daughters, Leah and Rachel. Several years later, with God's blessing, he decides to bring his wives and eleven sons back to Canaan, his homeland. Laban protests, but Jacob and his entire company sneak off by night. Laban pursues him but the two make a treaty not to harm each other. Then Jacob goes on his way, and the angels of God meet him when he camps that night.

> *³Jacob sent messengers ahead of him to his brother Esau in the land of Seir, the country of Edom. ⁴He instructed them: "This is what you are to say to my master Esau: 'Your servant Jacob says, I have been staying with Laban and have remained there till now. ⁵I have cattle and donkeys, sheep and goats, menservants and maidservants. Now I am sending this message to my lord that I may find favor in your eyes.' "*
>
> *⁶When the messengers returned to Jacob, they said, "We went to your brother Esau, and now he is coming to meet you, and four hundred men are with him."*
>
> *⁷In great fear and distress Jacob divided the people who were with him into two groups, and the flocks and herds and camels as well. ⁸He thought, "If Esau comes and attacks one group, the group that is left may escape."*
>
> *⁹Then Jacob prayed, "O God of my father Abraham, God of my father Isaac, O LORD who said to me, 'Go back to your country and your relatives, and I will*

make you prosper,' ¹⁰I am unworthy of all the kindness and faithfulness you have shown your servant. I had only my staff when I crossed this Jordan, but now I have become two groups. ¹¹Save me, I pray, from the hand of my brother Esau, for I am afraid he will come and attack me, and also the mothers with their children. ¹²But you have said, 'I will surely make you prosper and will make your descendants like the sand of the sea, which cannot be counted.' "

¹³He spent the night there, and from what he had with him he selected a gift for his brother Esau: ¹⁴two hundred female goats and twenty male goats, two hundred ewes and twenty rams, ¹⁵thirty female camels with their young, forty cows and ten bulls, and twenty female donkeys and ten male donkeys. ¹⁶He put them in the care of his servants, each herd by itself, and said to his servants, "Go ahead of me, and keep some space between the herds."

¹⁷He instructed the one in the lead, "When my brother Esau meets you and asks, 'To whom do you belong, and where are you going, and who owns all these animals in front of you?' ¹⁸then you are to say, 'They belong to your servant Jacob. They are a gift sent to my lord Esau, and he is coming behind us.' "

¹⁹He also instructed the second, the third, and all the others who followed the herds: "You are to say the same thing to Esau when you meet him. ²⁰And be sure to say, 'Your servant Jacob is coming behind us.' " For he thought, "I will pacify him with these gifts I am sending on ahead; later, when I see him, perhaps he will receive me." ²¹So Jacob's gifts went on ahead of him, but he himself spent the night in the camp.

Helpful Notes
- *Sent messengers ahead.* According to the *NIV Study Bible*, Esau's territory was well to the south of Jacob's ultimate destination. Jacob could have avoided meeting his brother. But instead, he assumes Esau will pursue him when he hears Jacob has left Laban. So Jacob takes the first step, hoping to head off trouble.

1. Nearly 20 years have passed since Jacob tricked Esau out of his birthright. Now, as the two are about to meet, what do you think is going through Jacob's

mind? What details show his attitude toward his brother?

2. When Jacob learns that Esau is headed his way with four hundred men, what does he do first? Next? What does this tell you about Jacob?

3. How would you describe Jacob's prayer?

4. After he prays, Jacob elaborately plans to send wave after wave of gifts to pacify his brother. Was this prudent, or does it reveal a lack of faith in God's provision and promise?

5. What can we learn from Jacob's example about laying the groundwork for reconciliation?

Continue the reader's theater format. No new readers are needed.

Read Genesis 33:1-12, 13-14, 16, 20. After spending a lonely night wrestling with God, Jacob meets Esau.

Jacob looked up and there was Esau, coming with his four hundred men; so he divided the children among Leah, Rachel, and the two maidservants. ²He put the maidservants and their children in front, Leah and her children next, and Rachel and Joseph in the rear. ³He himself went on ahead and bowed down to the ground seven times as he approached his brother.

⁴But Esau ran to meet Jacob and embraced him; he threw his arms around his neck and kissed him. And they wept. ⁵Then Esau looked up and saw the women and children. "Who are these with you?" he asked.

Jacob answered, "They are the children God has graciously given your servant."

⁶The maidservants and their children approached and bowed down.

⁷Next, Leah and her children came and bowed down. Last of all came Joseph and Rachel, and they too bowed down.

⁸Esau asked, "What do you mean by all these droves I met?"

"To find favor in your eyes, my lord," he said.

⁹But Esau said, "I already have plenty, my brother. Keep what you have for yourself."

¹⁰"No, please!" said Jacob. "If I have found favor in your eyes, accept this gift from me. For to see your face is like seeing the face of God, now that you have received me favorably. ⁱⁱPlease accept the present that was brought to you, for God has been gracious to me and I have all I need." And because Jacob insisted, Esau accepted it.

¹²Then Esau said, "Let us be on our way; I'll accompany you."

¹³But Jacob said to him, . . . ¹⁴". . . let my lord go on ahead of his servant, while I move along slowly at the pace of the droves and that of the children, until I come to my lord in Seir. . . ."

¹⁶So that day Esau started on his way back to Seir. . . . ¹⁸[Jacob] arrived safely at the city of Shechem in Canaan and camped within sight of the city. . . . ²⁰There he set up an altar and called it El Elohe Israel.

Helpful Notes
- *Bowed down . . . seven times.* This custom was a clear sign to Esau that Jacob was in total submission to him.
- *Until I come to my lord in Seir.* As the subsequent verses indicate, Jacob had no intention of meeting his brother in Seir. Even after the reconciliation, he doesn't trust Esau and he again resorts to deception.

1. Esau had wanted to kill Jacob. What changed his mind?
2. What did Jacob say, do, or think that promoted reconciliation? What about Esau?
3. How do you think this reconciliation affected Jacob, especially spiritually?

MAIN IDEAS

- God wants broken relationships to be healed.
- Reconciliation is a difficult process that requires determination, courage, humility, sincerity, forgiveness. It does not assign blame, rationalize earlier behavior, or set conditions.
- Prayer is an important part of the reconciliation process.
- The passing of time and growth in maturity may make reconciliation easier.

Leader: Have group members sum up the main ideas they've received from the session so far, or ask someone to read the summary below. Do the same for the "Good News" section.

- Restitution for wrongs committed in the past may be part of the reconciliation process.

GOOD NEWS

In Jesus Christ, God reconciles us to himself. And he empowers us to be agents of reconciliation in our own broken relationships.

REFLECTION TIME

5-7 minutes

> **Leader:** You might remind the group that these personal, written reflections can guide our prayers during the week as well as during this session.

1. What did I learn for which I can praise and thank God?

2. Is a significant relationship in my life, once characterized by closeness, now marked by hostility and distance? If so,

   - Am I motivated to be reconciled?
   - Do I need to confess that I contributed to the problem?
   - Can I claim a promise of God?
   - What can I do to begin the process of reconciliation?
   - For what should I ask God?

3. In the light of our study of reconciliation, how can the group pray for me?

PRAYER TIME

PREPARATION

5-7 minutes

We may hesitate to share with the group situations in which we needed to make things right between ourselves and others. On the other hand, talking about it—even without identifying specific individuals—can help. And praying about it, whether privately or publicly, is always right. Share as much as or little as you like of your answers to questions 1-3.

Leader: This may be a good time to talk about confidentiality—an absolute "must" for all group members.

PRAYER

10-15 minutes

Begin with a time of praise and thanks for the reconciliation that God has brought into your life and relationships. Feel free to read or recite a verse from the psalms or other passages as part of your praise and thanksgiving.

After the praise time, spend time in quiet prayer about the need for reconciliation in your life and relationships.

Then bring your prayers that you want to say aloud. Pray for yourself and for the needs of the group.

Close by singing or saying in unison "They'll Know We Are Christians by Our Love" or another song of your choice.

Before beginning your prayer time, you could read James 5:16 to the group: "Therefore confess your sins to each other and pray for each other so that you may be healed. The prayer of a righteous man is powerful and effective."

PLANNING FOR MINISTRY

Last week we suggested the group talk about a possible service project. Projects that attempt to bring about healing and reconciliation in your community would be a wonderful way to put today's session into action.

Session 7
REACHING OUT

OPENING SHARE TIME
10-15 minutes

Talking about our spiritual roots is an important way to grow in our relationships with each other. Question 2, below, gives you a chance to do that.

1. New experiences are harder for some than they are for others. How do you feel and what do you think when you walk into a new group?
2. How did you become a Christian? (Or, what is drawing you toward Christ today?)

> Leader: When discussing question two, talk especially about the role specific individuals (parents, friends, teachers, etc.) took in drawing members of your group to Christ.

BIBLE DISCOVERY TIME
20-30 minutes

Most of the time God works through people to accomplish his purposes in our lives. In this study we see two examples of God using people to reach out and touch others at their point of need.

> Ask one or two group members to read the introductory comments and the Bible passages. Lead the group in discussing the questions that follow the passages.

Read Acts 8:26-40. This passage describes how Philip reached out to an Ethiopian. Philip was a Jewish Christian first appointed as one of the original seven deacons of the church in Jerusalem. He later became an evangelist, bringing the good news and performing miracles in Samaria.

> *[26]Now an angel of the Lord said to Philip, "Go south to the road—the desert road—that goes down from Jerusalem to Gaza." [27]So he started out, and on his way he met an Ethiopian eunuch, an important official in charge of all the treasury of Candace, queen of the Ethiopians. This man had gone to Jerusalem to worship, [28]and on his way home was sitting in his chariot reading the book of Isaiah the prophet. [29]The Spirit told Philip, "Go to that chariot and stay near it."*
>
> *[30]Then Philip ran up to the chariot and heard the man reading Isaiah the prophet. "Do you understand what you are reading?" Philip asked.*

³¹ "How can I," he said, "unless someone explains it to me?" So he invited Philip to come up and sit with him.

³² The eunuch was reading this passage of Scripture:

"He was led like a sheep to the slaughter,
　and as a lamb before the shearer is silent,
　so he did not open his mouth.
³³ In his humiliation he was deprived of justice.
　Who can speak of his descendants?
　For his life was taken from the earth."

³⁴ The eunuch asked Philip, "Tell me, please, who is the prophet talking about, himself or someone else?" ³⁵ Then Philip began with that very passage of Scripture and told him the good news about Jesus.

³⁶ As they traveled along the road, they came to some water and the eunuch said, "Look, here is water. Why shouldn't I be baptized?" ³⁸ And he gave orders to stop the chariot. Then both Philip and the eunuch went down into the water and Philip baptized him. ³⁹ When they came up out of the water, the Spirit of the Lord suddenly took Philip away, and the eunuch did not see him again, but went on his way rejoicing. ⁴⁰ Philip, however, appeared at Azotus and traveled about, preaching the gospel in all the towns until he reached Caesarea.

Helpful Notes

- *Gone to Jerusalem to worship.* Apparently the Ethiopian eunuch was a Gentile believer in God.

> Leader: Refer to "Helpful Notes" when they pertain to your discussion. You may want to ask a group member to read these notes aloud.

1. In what ways are Philip and the Ethiopian similar? Different?

2. What is the role and responsibility of the angel of the Lord and the Spirit of the Lord in this passage?

3. What is Philip's role and responsibility?

4. How do you see yourself today

   - explaining the gospel to someone, as Philip did?
   - searching, perhaps in need of greater understanding, as the Ethiopian was?
   - worshiping in Jerusalem with the other Christians?
   - doing something else, somewhere else?

Read Acts 9:19-31. Saul, a leader of the persecution of the early church, had just experienced a dramatic conversion on his way to Damascus to arrest and imprison the Christians living there. Sheltered and then baptized by a disciple in Damascus named Ananias, Saul plunged into his new ministry.

> Saul spent several days with the disciples in Damascus. [20] At once he began to preach in the synagogues that Jesus is the Son of God. [21] All those who heard him were astonished and asked, "Isn't he the man who raised havoc in Jerusalem among those who call on the name? And hasn't he come here to take them as prisoners to the chief priests?" [22] Yet Saul grew more and more powerful and baffled the Jews living in Damascus by proving that Jesus is the Christ.
>
> [23] After many days had gone by, the Jews conspired to kill him, [24] but Saul learned of their plan. Day and night they kept close watch on the city gates in order to kill him. [25] But his followers took him by the night and lowered him in a basket through an opening in the wall.
>
> [26] When he came to Jerusalem, he tried to join the disciples, but they were all afraid of him, not believing that he really was a disciple. [27] But Barnabas took him and brought him to the apostles. He told them how Saul on his journey had seen the Lord and that the Lord had spoken to him, and how in Damascus he had preached fearlessly in the name of Jesus. [28] So Saul stayed with them and moved about freely in Jerusalem, speaking boldly in the name of the Lord. [29] He talked and debated with the Grecian Jews, but they tried to kill him. [30] When the brothers learned of this, they took him down to Caesarea and sent him off to Tarsus.
>
> [31] Then the church throughout Judea, Galilee, and Samaria enjoyed a time of peace. It was strengthened; and encouraged by the Holy Spirit, it grew in numbers, living in the fear of the Lord.

Leader: You may want to use a large map (or distribute Bibles with maps) to identify the location of the various areas mentioned in today's passages.

Helpful Notes
- *In the synagogues.* A large number of Jews lived in Damacus, an important trading center in the Roman province of Syria. Damascus was located about 150 miles north of Jerusalem.
- *Barnabas.* We first hear of Barnabas in Acts 4:36, where he is described as a Levite from Cyprus, an island in the eastern Mediterranean. He sold a field and gave the proceeds to the apostles. His name means "Son of Encouragement." In Acts 11:24, he is described as "a good man, full of the Holy Spirit and faith." Barnabas later became an important companion of Paul on his missionary journeys.

1. What do you think Saul felt and thought as he tried to join the disciples at Jerusalem?

2. Switch perspectives and imagine the thoughts and feelings of the disciples as they encountered Saul. What might be a comparable situation today?

3. What did Barnabas risk in befriending Saul? What methods did he use? Why did he do it? With what results?

4. If possible, describe someone who was a "Barnabas" to you on your spiritual journey. As an alternative, describe a time when you needed encouragement and wanted someone to reach out to you.

5. On a scale of 1-10, indicate
   - your personal focus.
   - the group's focus.

   INWARD   1 2 3 4 5 6 7 8 9 10   OUTWARD

6. What is a godly way to respond to an individual or group who will not permit you to bridge from being an "outsider" to being "one of them"?

7. What are the rewards of being a Barnabas, a voice of encouragement, to others?

MAIN IDEAS

- God gives us opportunities to share the gospel with others or to encourage them in their faith.
- New believers often need a "Barnabas" who will reach out and build bridges between themselves and others.
- The Holy Spirit is the primary actor in the process of conversion. We play a secondary role in response to his prompting.
- Reaching out to others takes effort and courage. God's Spirit equips us to do this.

> Leader: For variety, you may want to read the main ideas in unison. Do the same with the "Good News" section.

GOOD NEWS

Sharing the gospel and encouraging others in their faith brings great joy.

REFLECTION TIME

7-10 minutes

Jot down your personal reflections, using the questions below.

1. Who has reached out to me or encouraged me in my faith? Have I thanked God for such persons?

> Group members work individually during the reflection time. Jot down your own personal responses to the reflection questions.

2. Have I been open to the Spirit's using me to share the gospel or encourage someone in his or her faith? Do I need to confess anything in this area? Can I claim a promise of God?

3. Is the Holy Spirit prompting me to serve someone as a "Philip" or "Barnabas"? If so, how should I pray for this person?

4. In light of what we discussed today, how can the group pray for me?

PRAYER TIME

PREPARATION
5-7 minutes

Leader: Go around the circle, giving each group member an opportunity to share his or her response to one or two of the reflection questions.

You are invited to share any answers or parts of answers from questions 1-4.

PRAYER
10-15 minutes

Ask a group member to read through these guidelines before the prayer time begins. Be ready to make the transitions into the various parts of the prayer time, as needed.

Begin with prayers of thanks for those who led us to Christ or encouraged us on our faith journeys. Give thanks especially for the role of the Holy Spirit in these matters.

Move into a time of confession, during which you may pray silently or aloud for forgiveness for failing to witness to or encourage others.

Pray for the persons and the needs that group members have mentioned during the reflection time.

Close by singing "Spirit of the Living God" or a song of your choice.

PLANNING FOR MINISTRY

We encourage you to send your reactions to this material to

Acts 2 / Caring Connections
CRC Publications
2850 Kalamazoo Ave. SE
Grand Rapids, MI 49560

Thank you.

Today, group members probably mentioned certain individuals who need to hear the gospel or who need spiritual encouragement. Recall such persons now and agree to pray for these persons each day during the week. If many names are mentioned, divide them between group members.

Decide what you'll study next. Will you change location, schedule of meetings, leadership, or format? Evaluate your use of the *Acts 2* materials. Here are a few questions to consider as a group: Is the opening share time effective? Do the Bible discovery questions produce good discussion? Has the reflection and prayer time become a meaningful part of your meetings? Are you spending enough time in prayer as a group? Has planning for ministry become part of your group process?

Revisit your plans to invite new people to the group. The beginning of a new study is an excellent time to invite others to your group. You might also consider sponsoring a social event to which potential new members could be invited.

APPENDIX A

GROUP GOALS PLANNING SHEET

1. We plan for our group to grow and to spawn a new group by _____
   _____.

2. We plan to have an empty chair at every meeting and to pray for a person(s) to come and fill that chair. _____yes _____no

   How are we doing?

3. We plan to pray three or four times a week for each of the _____ unchurched persons we have identified.

   How are we doing?

4. We plan to invite, on an average, _____ new people each month.

   How are we doing?

5. We plan to sponsor _____ "fishing pool" events this year.

   How are we doing?

6. We plan to do _____ service projects this year.

   How are we doing?

7. Additional group goals:

   Special joys:

   Problem areas: